MAKING A LIVING

FROM YOUR BOOK

By Sylvester Murray

Published by Create Space Independent Publishing Platform (2017)

CreateSpace

4900 LaCross Road

North Charleston, SC 29406

USA

Printed in the United States of America

TABLE OF CONTENTS

CHAPTER ONE

WHAT IS A TRUE SELF-PUBLISHING COMPANY?

Self-publishing means, in a general way, that the author publishes the book themselves, and thus absorbs the cost of publishing the book. The advantage is that the author receives all the profit, but the disadvantage is that self-publishing has a stigma, largely because many authors have self-published poor quality books that could not compete with traditionally published books for a number of reasons, ranging from cheap paper and low quality printing to multiple typos.

Self-publishing has its degrees of what many consider legitimate self-publishing. A true self-published book, in many people's opinions, is a book where the author oversaw the entire production, from layout to printing, and where the author owns the ISBN number, printing the book under his or her own publishing company's name. While "vanity," "subsidy," and "POD" are terms often used in relation to self-publishing, they are more like half-sisters of self-publishing because another publisher besides the author is involved, even though the author fronts the costs.

If your self-published book sells well, it will have little or nothing to do with the publisher you used. However, when you need more books, the average vanity publisher will make two to five dollars on each book you print and they don't deserve a dime, because they have no money invested in your book. You paid for everything. If you have been taken in by one of these so-called vanity publishers, you will overpay for unnecessary services and more often than not, wind up with an inferior, poorly produced book. Most vanity publishers don't even require editing, but if you want an edit, they will charge you for editing that will not necessarily meet modern publishing industry standards

You may be asking, how can I avoid going with the wrong publisher? The answer is so simple, you won't believe it. There is one thing that makes it impossible for them to take advantage of you, one thing that completely ties their hands. It is a number, nothing else, just a number. You will need a second number for an eBook version of your paperback. I'm talking about International Standard Book Numbers, that thirteen digit number commonly referred to as the ISBN. It's the number you see on the barcode on the back of books. Booksellers use it to order books listed by their ISBN's in the Ingram database.

That curious number is the key to being a true self-publisher. If you, the author, own it, you are a true self-publisher. If your publisher owns it and "assigns" it to you, you are not a self-published author. You just paid somebody to publish your book. And there is no such thing as an assigned ISBN. You either own it or you don't, period. That brings us to the question of what a true self-publishing company is. Well, it's not what you think.

I'm going to come right out and say it: there is no such thing as a self-publishing company. There are self-published authors, but no self-publishing companies. Don't let it confuse you. A true self-publishing company is actually a self-publishing "facilitator." They facilitate, or help authors become self-published. True self-publishing facilitators will help any author who wants to use their own ISBN .

THE ADVANTAGES OF SELF-PUBLISHING

As long as the author makes producing a quality book a top priority, self-publishing can be not only a feasible choice, but it may even be the better choice over traditional publishing. Following are some advantages for why you might consider self-publishing.

Control of Production: Self-publishing your book gives you complete control of the production. Rather than sell your rights to a publisher who will then edit your book the way they see fit and decide when to publish your book - often two years down the road - and decide whether to continue to sell your book or take it off the shelves, the self-publisher has complete control over timing and production. Your publisher may want your book to be a coffee table, expensive hard back book, while you want an inexpensive paperback so you can sell more copies. If you self-publish, then you can produce it the way you want. You can also guarantee that your book never goes out of print by reprinting it as often as you like or the market demands. By contrast, publishers often cease printing books that are not bestsellers, and then authors have to wait years for their contracts to expire to buy back the rights of their own books. Having complete control over the entire publishing process and the lifespan of your book is perhaps the greatest benefit of self-publishing.

Print Runs: I've heard authors argue that traditional publishers will produce larger print runs than self-publishers. This is true. Even the smallest traditional publishers will often do a print run in the low thousands, while a self-published author who has to pay for the entire production themselves might find it difficult to print more than 500 or 1,000 copies. Of course, you want your book to reach as many people as possible, but if your publisher prints 3,000 books and only 1,000 sell, what is the advantage over you printing 1,000 and keeping all the profit for yourself? A large print run is the weakest argument for staying with traditonal publishing, since if the book sells well, the money from the profit from the first small print run can be used to pay for the second and third and larger ones.

Marketing: Traditional publishers are doing less and expecting authors to do more marketing for their books. Unless a book is considered a potential bestseller, and few are, little money will be spent on marketing. An author willing to go out and promote themselves can be as successful at marketing a book as a publisher and might even get a publisher's attention down the road. While traditional publishers do have more resources and outlets for promoting books, guerrilla marketing by an author can equal those efforts, if the author educates themselves on marketing and is willing to spend the time and energy. Authors can also find assistance from publicity companies, many of which are very affordable today.

Profit: Any author who thinks he or she is going to get rich off of publishing a book is in the wrong business. As far as profit goes, if an author has to help the publisher to market the book and is receiving 10 percent royalties, it makes more sense for the author to publish his own book and receive far greater profit.

CHAPTER 2

TIPS TO SELF-PUBLISHING SUCCESS

Despite all your efforts, you will still find some people who will be dismissive of your book if it is self-published. The best way to overcome these objections and sell more copies is to produce a quality book. Here are some final tips and "musts" to make your book competitive.

Have Your Book Professionally Edited: A good editor will do more than fix typos and punctuation and grammar. They will enhance your words to their best potential while retaining your voice and meaning. They will make sure you sound professional, don't repeat yourself, and ensure you appeal to the wider reading public.

Remember What Your Readers Want: Readers want to know "What's in it for me?" They don't care about your personal story unless it has something in it that will help them. You can enjoy writing, but if you write for you, and not for others, you aren't going to sell books.

Ensure Quality Production: Don't print pages off your printer and have them bound. Avoid comb bindings. Go to a professional printer that has experience printing books and knows all the ins and outs of what kind of paper to use and all the other details. Be sure also to hire a professional to do the layout of your book and to design your cover.

Learn from Marketing Experts: Books don't sell themselves, and books on bookstore shelves don't sell if people don't know they are there. You don't have to hire a full-time publicity agent, but join a publishing organization, attend publishing conferences, read publications in the industry, find out what works for others, get book reviews, and hire reputable marketing services that will help you spread the word. Your book won't sell unless you are out there selling it, and marketing experts can teach you how to sell it so that it interests people.

WHY SELF-PUBLISHING?

Are you planning to get your idea into a printed book? Do you think that it is one of the greatest achievements in your lifetime? Certainly, in this endeavor to publish a book, a publishing company can be an astonishing partner. The publisher contributes an important role in targeting the perfect work and collaborates with the writer on writing the best book possible.

Today, more writers are turning to self-publishing. Due to its multiple benefits, people now prefer to self-publish. Many times, self-publishers do not wish to give up control of their book at all. Publishers are interested in a say in the final draft of the book, from a book's cover to an editorial standpoint. When thought of as a business approach, publishers also wish to put forth control over the pricing, sales plan, marketing and distribution of the book to maximize their profit. The majority of writers select to control their work themselves, on both the business and artistic sides of publishing a book.

Besides the control issue, a writer prefers to self-publish a book for the benefits listed below:

- To maintain direct control of the customer list.
- To make the most of the earnings the book brings in. Authors who are contracted to publishers can get 10 to 15%, whereas an author who publishes books on their own can make up to 70% of sales of the books.
- To Lower publishing cost.
- To market to a particular, small demographic of readers.

Every writer is interested in every aspect associated with his or her book. That is why many writers want to try the publishing business and get their book into the market.

Many writers prefer to publish work on their own.

Self-publishing is gaining popularity, as it has become easier, and the success stories clearly speak about its benefits. It is essential to understand the concept clearly. Do invest time in any research and learn the pros and cons of self-publishing.

HOW TO BECOME A SELF-PUBLISHING BESTSELLER?

If you dream big about becoming the next bestselling author around the world, then it is essential to understand the process clearly. Many writers jump into this endeavor without having any knowledge about self publishing and they simply end up in the sales stats showing no sales of the book.

Keep in mind that the real world is much harder than you think. You can publish your book easily, making it available to every soul on the internet. However, it does not mean that you will be the best seller. Bear this in mind clearly. This will make your publishing endeavor comparatively easy and less painful.

SELF-PUBLISHING: WHAT CAN IT DO FOR YOU?

If you want to self publish a book, you can string your texts together with the help of a program. Will this type of self published book get the success? Unfortunately, it will not. In addition, your name and reputation will be related to low quality work. Rather, think about it carefully. Do the research. Plan the book and collect the needed material. Write well and present it in an appropriate format. While doing all this work, quality should be your main focus.

CHAPTER 3

CONCEPTS AND STEPS TO BE FOLLOWED
IN SELF PUBLISHING
AND USEFUL TIPS ON SELF PUBLISHING

Self-publishing is the process of publishing one's own work or material without the intervention of a third person or publishing house. Here the owner or author of books is solely responsible for all activities concerning the publishing of the book. The author would control various activities like designing the cover of the book, arranging the pages in order, fixing the price for the book, delivery, sales and public relations, etc.

Sometimes, the author may outsource these activities to a reliable outsourcing company which provides these services. In the early days, the self-publishing author faced many problems, including investing huge sums of money in buying bulk copies and in locating a proper place to stock the books. But nowadays, after the arrival of print-on-demand skill, the author would advertise their work in a different medium and it is sufficient to print the book only when they receive a demand. This concept allows them to save a considerable amount of money and avoid problems in storing their books.

CONCEPT OF PRINT ON DEMAND AND ITS BENEFITS

The main concept of Print-on-Demand is that the cost is related to printing only one copy of a book, and is a fixed price, irrespective of the quantity of the order. The setup costs are also less expensive when compared to offset printing.

The main benefits of the Print on Demand concept are:

• Technical arrangement is faster

• No need to keep the books in stock.

• Decreases the storeroom and maintenance costs.

• Situation of unsold books would not arise

THE STEPS TO BE FOLLOWED WHILE SELF PUBLISHING

Through a confined copier:

Get ready to face issues - Self Publishing a book requires a lot of inventiveness and constrains. You should be ready to face disappointments or dissatisfaction in bringing out your book to the public. Your only aim is to publish your work using your own efforts and you should get rid of all the issues you are facing along the way of self publishing.

Valid Reasons - While self publishing your book, you must have valid reasons for your desire to publish your book on your own efforts. You must also be aware of the reason for fixing the cost of the book. If you think that the reasons you possess are genuine, then proceed further.

Edit your work - Before self publishing your book, proofread and make corrections in your work. If possible, you could give a copy of your book to your trustworthy friends and get their review on the work. If you feel genuine in their suggestions, make appropriate corrections in your work.

Provide a good title - Provide a catchy title of your book to attract people to buy your book by seeing the title itself. Initially, only the title of your book alone would draw the customers towards your book.

Copyright your work - When you are self publishing your work, you claim copyright of your book clearly either at the front or back cover of the book or in a well-known location of your book. Follow the legal procedures in claiming the copyright by filling out the necessary copyright application forms. Claiming copyright would save your book from possible plagiarists.

Through a website:

There are numerous online publishers who will publish your work in print format or eBook format free of cost. You have to pay them only when you sell your book.

You are required to set up a program to upload your copy and have control of it. Digitize the contents of your book using Microsoft Word or Pages if not done previously. There are several self publishing websites providing these services and you can make use of those sites.

While self publishing your work online, make sure to give an attractive title to your book to increase sales. Also, edit your work and make necessary corrections before publishing online.

Upload your finished book. After the editing work is completed, choose a design for the cover for your book, the cost of the book and the type of the book. Once you complete all these works, your book is ready for publishing and you would become a self published author.

USEFUL TIPS ON SELF-PUBLISHING

Before your book goes for print, get a proof of your book. If you want to change the appearance of the book, you change it before paying for the total copies.

Engage an expert proofreader to proofread your book. This avoids getting a bad name for your work because of the mistakes in your presentation. Provide brief descriptions to your book to attract customers.

The promotion of your book mainly depends on the method of providing wide publicity for your book. Publicity is the main key to promote the sale of any product.

While purchasing a book, customers often look at the front cover, back cover and the table of contents of the book. You can even hire a graphic artist to make these pages attractive to get good dividends.

List your book on self publishing sites like Amazon.com and include your comments to ensure that the book is precise, well written and free of grammar errors. This allows the customers to make the decision to buy your book. Provide two copies of your book to Amazon.com for scanning and made obtainable on the search feature.

As marketing is the central activity of any product that allows people to understand and buy the product, you can market your book through press releases, articles and websites etc.

After writing a book, an author will have to decide whether they would publish it traditionally or self publish it. Most authors would just share their book to friends and family or post it on a website and have their book downloaded, for free!

But, isn't it better if a book gets published and a larger number of readers have access to the book and be able to appreciate your work? The easiest, most convenient way to do it is through Self Publishing. The number of authors self publishing their books is increasing nowadays.

HERE ARE SOME REASONS WHY PEOPLE CHOOSE THE SELF PUBLISHING PATH

• No more rejection letters

Why do you have to burden yourself with writing proposals to dozens of publishers and end up getting rejected? It will only make you feel your book is not worthy to be published. With self publishing, there is no waiting, no writing of synopsis of the story, no staring at the wall. You will just go straight ahead with publishing your book!

• You are in control

Traditional publishers revise your book to make it "better". You are the creator of your work. You are the author. Why would you let someone edit your novel for their own convenience? That is your story; idea; imagination and hard work. If you Self Publish your book, you have full control of your story. You will publish what you want to publish.

Most importantly, you own the copyright of your book. So you can sell, giveaway or bundle your book any way you want to, without having to get permission from your publisher!

• You may earn more profits

Self publishing your book may give you more profit compared to a traditional publisher. You should earn all the money after paying for marketing and book printing. A traditional publisher will pay you 10-15% of the sale price of your book. Remember you also control the price of your book, so you determine how much profit you make for each book you sell.

CHAPTER 4

YOUR BOOK IS YOUR OWN WORK

You are in charge of your book. Whatever you want to do with it, do it! No one will stop you. Write whatever you want. Design the cover the way you want it. It's all you. You make all the decisions in your book from start to finish. A good self publishing company will be there only to provide you with publishing services, that's it.

BOOK EDITING

Book reading is more popular today than it ever was due to the fact that books are everywhere. They are more easily accessible to everyone and they are relatively inexpensive. Fiction has always been one of the top read genres but non-fiction is catching up, with more and more people opting to read this type of book. Just as popular as reading is book publishing, and today it is a bigger deal than ever because so many people are reading. One aspect of publishing that is maybe the most important thing when putting out a new book is editing. With more and more people becoming more educated than anyone was in the past, most readers, not just perfectionists, notice when there are mistakes in the book they are reading and they are likely to form a more negative reaction towards the particular publisher and/or editor.

There are several different types of editing:

1) Book Editing

2) Copyediting

3) Technical Editing

Book editing is a very crucial step in the process of bringing a book to life. Sending a book out into the world and expecting people to buy it and respond to it positively, even though there are mistakes in the manuscript, is a very big mistake. Book editing is just one step lower than proofreading because editing can bring in a lot of typographical errors to the manuscript. There are several types of book editing. The first type is hard editing, which refers to major changes being made to a specific work. Whole paragraphs may be reframed while keeping the meaning constant but explaining the concept better. This type of editing is also used to omit redundant matter or make an exceptionally long book shorter.

The purpose of copyediting is to improve grammatical correctness, political correctness, punctuation, terminology and factual correctness without changing the meaning of what is being said in works of non-fiction.

Works of non-fiction often times require the talents of a technical editor to edit things like computer codes and algorithms if they and similar things are included in the book. Usually, it is best to have someone who is not only a great technical editor but an expert in the field they are editing.

One of the biggest problems that comes with editing, in particular when it is the writer themselves that is doing the editing, is the writer becomes too attached to what they wrote and do not want to change it. After all, it is their idea, their creativity on the pages. A problem that can arise between writer and editor is the writer may become too vocal in what they want the editor to do and not do and this can cause friction between all parties involved. It is a good idea to never edit your own book and if you have issues with the way an editor is editing your work, subtly give suggestions and explain why a certain passage is written the way it is and why it would change it's meaning if it were to be rewritten a different way.

CHAPTER 5

HOW TO GO ABOUT PROMOTING YOUR BOOK

Promoting your book doesn't have to be a daunting task. It can be fun, but must be executed with precise planning. Promoting a book in the proper manner will generate interest. People will start buying the book, and you will reap the benefits of your hard work through money and popularity. When promoting your book, the possibilities are endless. The more creative your methods are, the more likely you are to catch people's attention.

One of the most important things about promoting your book, no matter how you went about having it published, is to always have a few copies on hand. Keep a few in your car when out running errands or traveling. And be sure that in case you run out of on hand copies, that you have a way for people to order your books.

One of the best methods to get attention is to start distributing complementary copies of the book. People love freebies, especially when it comes in the form of a gripping murder mystery or a sensual romantic escapade.

If the book is good enough, news will spread and people will buy the book. If you have copies to spare, you can leave sample books in your favorite coffee shops with flyers. The book may disappear, but giving it away is a good way to promote your book, because it gets people reading and talking about it.

You will have to begin with distributing pamphlets and mass-advertising sessions. This is going to cost you money but like the saying goes - nothing ventured, nothing gained.

Book signings are another great way to promote your new book. But try to think outside the box. Book signings don't have to be in a bookstore. Depending on what your book is about, try a specialty store. An example would be if you wrote a book on healthy cooking, try a book signing at a health food store. To arrange a book signing, try speaking with the manager of the place you want to sign at. In addition to having books to sign and sell, have a little write up on you and your book along with how people can go about ordering it.

Radio and newspaper interviews can also help promote your book. There are always empty spots on radio and in newspapers that need to be filled, so why not speak with your local radio station or newspaper to see if you can help them out. Send reviews to local and national magazines.

Participate in book fairs. Also, try local fairs in your area like health fairs, job fairs, etc. that focus on the theme of your book.

Optimize your web presence. If you do not know how, learn! It is becoming increasingly important to get internet exposure. There are many people who will hear the title of your book when a friend talks about it, and then decide to look it up online - and if they can't find it, you have likely just lost a reader. Not only that, but offering your book online makes it possible for anyone anywhere in the world to find your book.

Get on Amazon.com, and promote your book there. There is a "real name" feature that people can use to link back to your book. Write reviews on similar books and get into discussions. Be seen, and get attention that will lead back to your book. Having your book listed on Amazon is really the easiest way to ensure that there are always copies available. Most people who use the internet are at least a little familiar with Amazon and will be able to get your book delivered to them quickly.

Get a website! This is very important. You need a website as soon as your book is out. Also, if you have a website dedicated to the book, and ordering available on the website, this is a great way to promote your book. Create a promotional website for the book. Domain names can be created for as low as $9 per year. Once the domain is created, it is best to fill it with excerpts from the book along with testimonials from respected authorities. Ensure that the URL of the domain is included as the signature in your emails and posts on discussion boards. You need to connect your website directly to your book's page on many sites i.e. Amazon.

Post comments to blogs and websites that are related to your book. Promote your book in your comments, if appropriate, and hyperlink to your book's website from your signature. Refrain from joining forums with the sole intention of promoting the book! In order for forum advertising to be effective, you need to become a valued member of the community.

Ask people you know who have blogs to write reviews of your book on their blog sites. Your friends and family can help to promote your book by using their blogs and websites to spread the word.

Utilize social networking sites such as Facebook, Twitter, MySpace, etc. Create a fan page and post book excerpts as well as news & updates. Do not forget to join other fan pages & groups to network with other fans.

Follow your book's ranking on online ranking sites, especially sites that allow for reviews and comments. That may help you guide your book's marketing strategy, so you can promote your book to the best possible audiences.

Create a catchy video about your book, and don't forget to show your actual book so that people can see what it looks like. Often people will remember what a cover looks like when they can't even remember the title.

Above all, have fun. Promoting your book is a great way to share yourself with the world, so enjoy it.

There are many resources available to market your book. The most important thing to remember is that you are the best publicist for your work. It's your words and ideas, so you are the best person to promote your book.

BOOK MARKETING PLAN

To promote your book successfully, it's important to budget funds for book marketing. While it's certainly possible to do online book promotion on a shoestring budget, you will still need to invest in promoting your book.

Listed below is a list of the costs you may encounter when promoting your book:

Blog/Website: Website design and hosting fees. If you use a blog-based website, you'll minimize costs for online book promotion.

Graphics: Design of website header and graphics, design of printed materials, purchase of stock images for blog/website, and a photo shoot for your author photo.

Printing: Business cards, bookmarks, postcards, flyers, and posters for personal appearances. In addition to local printers, check prices for online printers such as Printing for Less.

Copywriting and Editing: You may want to hire a professional copywriter to help you write effective sales ideas for your website and other book promotion materials. It's also a good idea to have an editor or proofreader review your website and marketing materials.

E-mail Marketing: You will pay monthly or per mailing fees to the company that manages your opt-in mailing list.

Review Copies: Printing, packaging and postage for review copies sent through the mail.

Publicity: There are a number of free online press release services, such as PRLog and Free Press Release. To get wider distribution for your most important releases, you will need to use a paid service .

Learning: There are a number of blogs and newsletters with helpful book marketing information. But don't forget to budget funds for books, teleclasses and other opportunities to get more in-depth education about publishing and book marketing, and for dues to writing and publishing organizations. You'll be more effective at promoting your book if you know how to do it properly.

Administrative: You may need help in implementing your book marketing plan, especially if you have a day job. There are a number of virtual assistants who specialize in working with authors. You may also want to invest in consulting services from a publishing or book marketing coach to help you develop your book promotion strategy.

Other Expenses: Additional expenses may include travel, book fairs, book award entry fees, advertising, and administrative expenses such as postage and internet access.

BOOK PROMOTION –IMPORTANCE OF BLOGGING IN PROMOTING YOUR BOOK

Blogging is a terrific book promotion tool for authors. Here are eight ideas for using blogging in social and interactive ways to enhance your author platform and engage your readers:

1. Encourage your readers to share your content with others.

Make it easy for readers to share your content by adding "share" buttons from sites such as Share This or Add This. Then ask readers to share by including text at the end of your best posts such as: "Do you know someone who might benefit from these tips? Just click the Share This button below to send a link by email or recommend this post on your favorite social media sites."

2. Actively solicit comments.

Get readers engaged by including a sentence at the end of some posts inviting comments. Thank each commenter and make a further comment based on what they said.

3. Make comments on other blogs.

Making insightful comments on related blogs is a great book promotion tactic. Comments boost your visibility and create links and traffic to your site. Subscribe to the top blogs related to your book's topic or audience and watch for posts that you can comment on. Also, set up Google Alerts for your main keywords to stay on top of other relevant blog posts. Comments should be helpful and relevant -- be subtle about promoting your book.

4. Write guest posts for other blogs.

Another effective book promotion strategy is to contact other bloggers that cater to your audience and offer to write a guest article. Include a brief bio and a low-resolution photo. Search for relevant blogs on Google Blog Search.

5. Create a feed for your blog.

RSS feeds allow your blog posts to be automatically delivered to your visitors and to other websites. This benefits your book promotion by creating regular readers for your blog, rather than relying on drop-in traffic.

6. Do a virtual book tour.

As part of your book promotion strategy, make guest appearances on blogs or podcasts to promote your book within a specific time frame - usually one to two weeks. Provide unique content to each host on your tour. Content can include interviews, how-to articles, book excerpts, videos, book reviews, or an article about how you developed the plot or characters for a novel.

7. Join a blog carnival.

Blog carnivals are a collection of links pointing to blog posts on a particular topic, or topics of interest to a particular group of people. Learn more at Blog Carnival.

8. Hold a contest or drawing on your blog.

Use the blog comment feature to hold contests. For example, post a question and award a prize to the first person who leaves a comment with the correct answer. Or, write a blog post stating that everyone who leaves a comment on the post by a specific date (allow five to seven days) will be entered in a drawing to win a free copy of your book. Promote the contest on your social networks.

PROMOTE YOUR BOOK ON TWITTER

Twitter, the wildly popular micro-blogging site, is a great place to network with others and subtly promote your book. Here are ten ways authors can benefit from Twitter:

1. Help others by sharing information, while you gain a reputation as an expert. You can post links to helpful articles, recommend resources, and teach mini-lessons. It is okay to link to your own blog posts and articles, but don't make that your main focus.

2. Meet potential customers and stay in touch with existing customers. Promote your Twitter URL everywhere you're listed online, and include keywords in your tweets to attract followers who are interested in your topic or genre.

3. Stay on top of news and trends in your field, and get ideas for your own articles and blog posts by reading the tweets of the people you follow.

4. Promote your book by tweeting about live and virtual events such as book signings, podcasts, virtual book tours, teleseminars, and book launches.

5. Gain visibility and new followers by hosting a Twitter contest where you give away a prize to a randomly chosen winner, or give a free gift to everyone who follows you and re-tweets your contest message. See this article for tips on creating a Twitter contest.

6. Ask for help and get instant responses. When you request product recommendations, referrals to experts, or help with a technical issue, it's amazing how helpful folks are.

7. Spread good will by promoting your peers. Introduce other people in your field or genre, or recommend other related books or products. Re-tweet interesting posts from people that you follow.

8. Promote your book and other products and services. The key is to be subtle and make promotional tweets a small percentage of your overall communications, so people feel like they gain value from following you, not just a stream of sales pitches.

9. Meet other authors, experts, publishers, marketers, and vendors. Twitter is ideal for networking and it's a great place to meet potential joint venture partners that can help you promote your book.

10. Keep in touch when you're on the road. There are a number of applications that facilitate twittering from mobile devices.

BOOK PRESS RELEASE - PROMOTE A BOOK ON THE WEB

It pays to be versatile.

Press releases can be used to promote almost anything. Whether you are looking to release a product, offer a service, or hold an event, you will find that a press release addresses a huge part of your promotional needs. For book promotion, the press release is particularly suitable.

If that's not great enough, press releases are simple to write and easy to distribute, with the added benefit of the service being made available for free in many cases. With all these advantages, it's not surprising that more and more people are turning to press releases to promote their books, especially as writers often do not have much of a marketing budget. Combined with the wide reach and speed of the internet, the press release can be highly effective in promoting your book.

THE POWER OF THE PRESS RELEASE

Book press releases often answer the basic questions of who, what, when, where, and how associated with your book. As a writer, you will be well able to find an interesting angle on the book that you have written. Remember that your press release is not meant to be a hard sell of your book. It needs to provide an impartial, newsworthy and interesting account of aspects of your book so that the reader wants to learn more.

On another note, press releases may also use different perspectives although still centered around the same product, service, or event. For example, in promoting your book, you can write different press releases on different aspects of it. One may be about the book itself, detailing the gist of the plot plus information about how readers can get their copy, while another may be about the launch of the book..

Using this strategy, you will soon have as many press releases on your book as you have time to write and you should never run out of ideas. Have each press release posted in a different place with a link back to your web site or sales page and you will already be thinking like a professional book promoter. Even when you don't really have different things to promote, such as the example of the book and a book launch, you can still create different press releases by changing your content and picking out different ways of looking at your book. I favor posting unique press releases each time that are not published anywhere else, because they make your promotional efforts more dynamic and avoid duplicate content, which is the bane of search engines. Don't forget to assign the right tags and categories so that your press releases will be picked up by your targeted audience.

CHAPTER 6

TRADITIONAL PUBLISHING

The only way you could get your book published traditionally was to have a publishing company offer you a contract. With this traditional method, in return for providing editing, proofing, design and printing as well as guidance and experience at no cost to the author, an author gives away any rights and control of their book to the publisher. The publisher makes their own decisions as to editing and cover choices, often times effecting changes that the author may not agree with. While an author may have some input, the final decision is up to the publisher, which often causes friction between publisher and author.

While the author argued that it was necessary to be true to the story, the publisher looked to the bottom line, for example believing that Caucasians would not buy a book with a person of color on its cover. Because the author gave up their rights to the book, the publisher had the final say. But the times may be changing.

In exchange for giving up all rights to their book, the publishing company pays an author an advance against future royalties that may or may not be earned back by the sale of the book. This advance can be anywhere from a few hundred to millions of dollars if you are already a best selling author. While smaller presses are more likely to give new writers a chance, that chance would be reflected in a smaller advance offered to an author. But no matter how large or small the advance, this advance is not "free" money to the author, as the publishing company deducts future royalties out of the advance until the publisher has recouped its investment.

With traditional publishers, the publishing company is betting the book will sell, at a minimum, enough copies to cover the advance, so the size of the advance is based upon the number of books the publisher thinks it can sell to cover its costs. If a book does not sell, the publisher would be out the advance they paid the author and they will not get their costs covered. If the book does sell, the publisher's costs are covered, their advance is paid off and future sales bring in money not only for the publisher but for the author as they begin to get ongoing royalties. However, these royalties are only a very small percentage from the sale of each book, usually on average around seven percent. Therefore, for an author to actually make money from their book, there has to be a large number of book sales.

Generally, to have a chance at being picked up by a traditional publisher, an author needs an agent. Publishers receive numerous unsolicited manuscripts all the time. Many unsolicited manuscripts are not ready for publishing or are not marketable in their current state so they are not considered at all. While generally editors will look at all these manuscripts and actually read a few, the chances of being "discovered" among all the unsolicited manuscripts are slim to none. However, an agent has the experience to know what can be a successful manuscript and will personally submit a work to any number of publishers in hopes of receiving an initial positive response.

In order to obtain an agent and subsequently a publisher, an author will have to put together an all-embracing book proposal. This can be very time consuming and expensive if the author hires someone else to do it for them, and not necessarily successful if a writer decides to do it themselves. Then, assuming the author hires an agent, and the agent gets a publishing company to go forward with the manuscript, the agent negotiates a publishing contract. Chances are, most authors will not get a huge advance on their first book as the publishing company wants to see how successful a new writer can be. There are always exceptions, but for the average author, it is best not to plan on making a living on their first book. However, an author with a publishing contract will not have to come up with any money to get their book published.

If an author is published by a traditional publishing company, they will automatically have credibility as an expert with the prestige that goes along with that. The publisher will help with marketing and distribution of the book, providing some publicity support. They will get the book into stores. Sometimes the company will even set up opportunities for the author for speaking engagements and book signings. However, unless the author is very well known, this media exposure may only last for a couple of months. Even with a traditional publisher, for an author to prove their worth by sales (which will translate to bigger advances for a second book), they must be willing to put in time, effort and money to promote their own book in addition to any efforts by the publisher.

TRADITIONAL PUBLISHING VERSUS SELF-PUBLISHING

As a writer, you probably are confused as to whether to try to get your book published traditionally by a commercial publisher or to self-publish. To make your decision a bit easier, consider your goals and expectations, as well as the following six points.

Acceptance

A large commercial publisher will not consider a manuscript unless it is represented by a literary agent. While some small independent presses do accept "unagented" manuscripts, that door is closing fast, since the number of independent presses has shrunk by 50 percent in the last decade. Your query letter and synopsis are critical in getting the attention of literary agents. Because literary agents get 200+ queries a month, it is not surprising that 99 percent of submissions are rejected. Yet many rejected manuscripts are worthy of publication, as self-publishing authors are discovering. On the other hand, since self-publishing is open to anyone, there is a flood of low quality books that will have little or no readership, giving self-publication a bad reputation.

Control

Once you sign with a traditional publisher, you lose some or most control of your manuscript. The publisher has influence over the title, the cover, the content, the pricing, the promotion, distribution, and timing of the aforementioned--and may hold some copyright--as determined by your specific contract. With self-publishing, you retain control of your manuscript.

Upfront Costs

A traditional publisher does not require you to pay any printing costs. In addition, you should not pay any costs to your literary agent before the sale of the manuscript to a publisher. Your agent makes his/her money (usually 15%) as a percentage of the advance (if any) and sale of your book. With self-publishing, you bear all the publication costs for formatting and distributing your book. The cost varies depending on the vendor and services you choose. A vendor may try to "upsell" you on editing, cover design, marketing, publicity, etc. Realize, most vendors make their money by selling extra services you may not need.

Turnaround Time

On average, a traditional publisher requires 12-18 months to publish your book. Figure another 6-12 months to secure a literary agent (if you can). So with traditional publishing, your manuscript will not see the "light of day" for a long time. In addition, with all the publishing acquisitions by global enterprises, your project could get caught in the middle of a merger and be abandoned altogether. With self-publishing, you can have your book overnight in some cases.

Book Store Presence

With self-publishing, getting your book into bookstores is extremely difficult. One reason is that bookstores work on a business model that requires they return unsold books to the publisher--and they don't want to deal with individual authors. If you have your heart set on seeing your book in Barnes and Noble or Borders stores, self-publishing is not for you.

Promotion and Selling

Regardless of how you publish your book, you are responsible for promoting and selling it. New writers are often surprised to learn that commercial publishers do not actively market and promote their books and that they expect their authors to do the work.

Royalties

A traditional publisher normally pays 15% royalty on book sales--plus your literary agent gets 15% of your royalties. When you self-publish, you earn a higher profit (25-100%). The amount you receive depends on how you sell your book and can be complicated by several layers of distribution fees.

The key to getting your book published successfully is to match your realistic expectations with publishing industry requirements and costs. Regardless of your decision, be sure your manuscript is in tip-top shape, having been professionally edited, before you submit to literary agents or embark on self-publishing.

WHAT ARE THE DIFFERENCES BETWEEN TRADITIONAL PUBLISHING AND SELF-PUBLISHING ?

Traditional publishing is a lengthy process of courtship between author, agent, and publisher. First the author writes the manuscript. They then try to get an agent, which is a monumental task in and of itself. Once represented, the author writes a query or a proposal and submits it to a publishing house through the procured agent. The publishing house then either accepts or rejects the author's work. If accepted, the publishing house buys the rights to the work from the writer and pays an advance on royalties. The publishing house decides when to publish the book, zealously edits the content, selects the cover design, prints the predicted number they think will sell, and then distributes the book to its contracted book sellers. Once the book is distributed, the publisher may or may not actively promote the book. The total sales dictate the percentage royalty the author earns. Many authors are surprised to discover that once the book is distributed, the author is expected to promote at their own expense. If a book does not sell as well as expected in the first 120 days, some publishing houses require the author to return their advance. However, if successful you could be the next Stephen King or John Gresham.

If the author's query is refused, they are then free to take it to another publisher. The reality of the query process is that a writer with a good, clean, well-written and well-edited manuscript will make the rounds at many different publishing houses before they are successful. The process can take years and requires incredible persistence as each publisher can take up to six months to generate a letter of rejection.

Self-publishing is often seen as the red-headed step-child of the literary world. There is a stigma associated with self-publishing in some circles; however, for many budding authors, it is their saving grace. Once in print and on the bookseller's shelf, the average reader cannot discern a self-published book from one that has been traditionally published.

When pursuing self-publishing, the author becomes their own publisher. The author must not only write the book but must also pay for the cover design, the editing, the printing, the advertising, and the distribution as well. They must be prepared to market, fill orders, and run their own public relations campaign, too. The author owns their work outright and an aggressive promoter can sell their way to the best seller list with a good sales strategy that includes a powerful website to boost and support sales. The good news is that the author can have the book in their hands in 6 months from a completed manuscript as opposed to traditional publishing which takes more than a year!

However, you get what you pay for in the process of self publishing . It is your book, your cover, and your content. There are some drawbacks to self-publishing that go beyond the expensive initial outlay. Publishing and promoting your book will be very time consuming. It requires a unique blend of marketing and business savvy that most authors do not have to start with but quickly become adept in the processes. Most of the work associated with getting a book successfully marketed and in the hands of the public requires performing tasks totally unrelated to writing.

CHAPTER 7

WHAT IS THE IMPORTANCE
OF SOCIAL MEDIA MARKETING?

In the world of technology, communication has become easier than ever. The world has now shrunk from a vast populated land to a network of communicating individuals living in a global village. People from all over the globe have come closer together and distances have decreased to the extent that an individual is merely a click away.

In this ever-growing network of people, a new theory has emerged, the idea of 6 degrees of separation. The idea behind this is that between you and any another person in the world is only a chain no longer than six people. This emphasizes the significance of online communication and the way it has made the world a whole lot smaller.

This is the power of social media and the developments in online communication. A happening in one part of the world reaches to the second part in a matter of seconds. Imagine if that news or happening was about you. The significance of this technology is the ease it provides. Using this tool to your advantage can give you a large number of benefits.

• Social Media Marketing brings global fame to your name.

This is your ticket to international level fame. Your company or your name could be known throughout the globe with millions of followers and fans. Millions of people can access these sites where people come to communicate online and express their views. Once you step into the world of social media marketing, all of these people become your potential prospects. Your services are merely a single search away.

• Promote your business or product as a serious product.

This technology provides you access to virtually the whole world and all its inhabitants. They are there to read and share anything that you have to say. This is your chance to establish an image for yourself that says "Hey! I am here to do business" and "I am serious about the product or services that I provide".

• Brings you closer to thousands of people without much effort.

Social media marketing is practically free. If you were to attempt to reach out to millions of people through physical means, you would have to make a lot of investments. This technology is the way to most efficiently reach out to your potential clients, not only in terms of finances but in terms of time as well.

• Gives you feedback on the type of viewer you have.

An interesting thing about marketing on these social websites is the level of feedback that you can expect. Using social media marketing can in fact educate you about the people who are or might be interested in your product or service. This gives you a better chance of altering your campaigns to gain improved results. You may learn about the number of people who visit your page, or the ages of people who comment or share your posts, or even their ethnicities, localities, religion, hobbies and preferences. You educate the world about your product and social media marketing educates you about the people who take interest in it. You get to know them personally through the network of social media.

• Makes you more accessible.

Social media sites ensure your presence 24 hours a day, 7 days a week. Your client can easily drop off a message and you can choose to reply as soon as you wish. This strengthens the bond between you and your customer and inspires a feeling of loyalty for your brand. This constant availability cannot be found when dealing with a physical office due to office opening and closing times. This ease for the customers to reach out to you in their time of need can only be ensured by social media.

• Social media levels the playing field.

Whether you are a multinational company or a single person start-up, in the world of social media you are all on the same level. Your finances and resources may not make much of a difference when it comes to social media. What does make a difference is your skill to communicate and attract people and the quality of the product or services that you provide. In the physical world, new start-ups would face immense financial difficulties in trying to promote themselves, while the marketing of giant enterprises would continue to dominate. Social media network gives you a fair playing field to show your true spirit and skill.

• You might discover new potential clients or customers.

While reviewing your feedback from viewers, you might begin to see obvious patterns in your business response. People from a particular region that you might never have thought of, who are showing a lot of interest in your product, are your best clients. These patterns will also allow you to see certain untapped markets that you can exploit. You can swiftly move and make use of the opportunity.

• Marketing campaign is easier to manage and cost-effective.

Setting up a social media marketing campaign requires much less effort than actually setting out to physically execute your marketing campaign, for example putting up banners or advertisements etc. in order to get your message across. Social media marketing is relatively easy to manage and quite frequently updated.

CHAPTER 8

TARGETING YOUR BOOK

Marketing your new Kindle book is the same as marketing anything else. The first thing you have to do is to figure out who exactly you are selling your book to. Don't spend any money advertising your book unless you know the precise target audience. Who, in your mind, will be the average buyer? Who will find your book interesting ?

One of the best and most affordable ways to find book buyers is by finding bloggers that review the type of book you've written. This can generate almost instant sales, especially if the reviews are positive. Below are some tips to make this happen for you:

The first thing you need is a list of reviewers online. Many of these people are located online, and lists and directories can be found by doing a simple search on Google. Make sure the reviewers on the list normally review books by small or self-published authors.

After finding a suitable list, break it down by reviewers who have reviewed books in your category. If the reviewer usually writes on romance novels, then their audience probably won't buy your crime fiction novel. If their preference is not listed in your directory, read through some of their reviews to see what they focus on.

Write an individual email to each reviewer, but before doing this, make sure you know their review terms and conditions. Some want books in different formats, and some do not review eBooks.

When you are ready to write your emails, be sure to make them as professional as you can. A sloppy email probably means they won't even give your book a glance. An average email, depending on each reviewer's conditions, will have your books title and genre, the format your book is available in, when the book will be available in other formats or print, what format they usually like, summary of your book, and anything more that they require. Be sure to thank them and include all of your contact information at the end of the email.

Be sure to get back to them as quickly as possible if and when they respond. If they want an electronic copy, send it right away. If they want a print copy and you can supply, send it the next morning or sooner.

Don't be discouraged if not everyone gets back to you. Also, if someone responds and says they want to review your book but have a long queue, have patience. While it won't help sales initially, it might give you a bunch of new sales and fans when they do review it. Patience is extremely important, especially when you are a new author.

Being a writer can be frustrating, but with a little persistence and knowledge, you should be able to get your book off the ground. Follow the tips above to help you get going in the right direction and with a quality Kindle book you will start to see sales coming in

HOW TO START MARKETING YOUR BOOK

Imagine if you could immediately sell 1,000 or 5,000 copies of your book in one sale. Most authors don't believe that it can be done, but it can be, and it is. Whether you are a first-time author or a best-selling author, you could be taking advantage of alternative distribution channels to unload large amounts of your book at a huge profit.

The non-retail sector of the book market is enormous and one that many authors rely on more for their profits than traditional sales. This sector includes many different types of organizations - from the government to the military, from nationwide conventions to non-profit organizations. Marketing your book through these channels is much easier and quicker than relying on one sale at a time.

You have probably been on the receiving end of these book marketing techniques, but you didn't even know it. When you go to a convention and are given a gift bag of pens, key chains, and notepads, there are often one or two books in there, too. These books are sometimes given to the convention to promote the other product, while other times these books are sold to the convention to be given to the attendees.

Marketing your book in this way enables you to quickly introduce yourself and your writing to a large group of people who you already know are interested in your product, service, or ideas. Once they have read your book, or seen your name, they will likely want to read more.

Non-profit organizations and professional associations are also good targets for marketing your book. You can easily personalize your book to their organization which will make it even more valuable to all the people who receive it. This is one of the easiest ways to begin marketing your book and establishing yourself as a respected author.

www.ingramcontent.com/pod-product-compliance
Lightning Source LLC
Chambersburg PA
CBHW070828260726
48654CB00024B/543